Native Language

poems by

Michael Beebe

Finishing Line Press
Georgetown, Kentucky

Native Language

Copyright © 2025 by Michael Beebe
ISBN 979-8-88838-947-8 First Edition
All rights reserved under International and Pan-American Copyright Conventions. No part of this book may be reproduced in any manner whatsoever without written permission from the publisher, except in the case of brief quotations embodied in critical articles and reviews.

Publisher: Leah Huete de Maines
Editor: Christen Kincaid
Cover Art: Michael Beebe
Author Photo: Michael Beebe
Cover Design: Elizabeth Maines McCleavy

Order online: www.finishinglinepress.com
also available on amazon.com

Author inquiries and mail orders:
Finishing Line Press
PO Box 1626
Georgetown, Kentucky 40324
USA

Contents

I

The Day Then Gone 1
We So Long Unknowing 2
Voice 3
Marine Layer 4
After Reading Quantum Theory 5
Well-Articulated Before All Description 6
Nobska Beach 7
The Argument from Perfections 8
Mountain Home 9
Straightening Nails 10
Picture of the Bride and Groom 11
Feeding the Quail 12
Camellias in Spring 13
The Afternoon is Late, and the Light is Old 14
The Falling Rain, the Slant of Light 15
In One's Native Language 16
Antonello's St. Jerome 17
The Vision of Reason 18
Right There All There 19
In This Open 20

II

The Day Like a Struck Bell 23
Even Only at the Office 24
Tonight, and Again Tomorrow 25
Failing to Find Your Public Face 26
In That Felt Absence 27
On Being Anguished in Marin County 28

Political Poem 29
What Happened Today 30
What We Do Hear, and Don't 31
Reading the Medievals 32
Here I Am Again 33
How After Darwin 34
Kant and Freud 35
Aristotle and Newton 36
The Wet Brown and Green 37
Witness 38
Plague Poem with Climate Change 39

III

In Snow and Mountains 43
You Had Thought it Was a Unity 44
Turning Your Back 45
How When a Very Bad Thing Happens 46
Bending Slowly Forward from the Waist 47
Pathology Report 48
In Extremis 49
"But What if He Dies?" 50
Aftermath 51
More Die of Heartbreak 52
Morning in Late Fall 53
Sensing and Sensed 54
Again In the Rain 55
And We Walking Away 56
Hands' Desire 57
Sailing to Alexandria 58
Attending the Good 59
December 31st 60

I

The Day Then Gone

When I got home from work that night
I found I was grieving, for the day then gone,
its sun or rain, its sound and step and place,
never to be again in all of time or space or beyond.

I tried but could not remember what the day was like,
what the slant of sun showed, the movement of cloud, where
the bird sang, how the light changed and changed again
while I drove to work that morning.

As if remembering could preserve the day and all the days before,
as if right attention could fix and keep that immensity of detail,
the ungraspable, utterly contingent multiplicity of the all of all,

Of things unique, particular, held here in the hand
or far in the depths infinite and infinitesimal,
each moment now never to be again.

We So Long Unknowing

We have left the farm behind,
vegetables and cows and wheat fields,
dirt and snow and sun and rain,
all the old life.

We looked up, paused, then said "Now."
Gathered our things, made our goodbyes,
set out on the road beyond our door,
went up into the ships.

We had waited these many years,
yearned for word from the others before,
now we too have gone.

But the voyage has been so long,
so long since we left the farm behind,
we so long unknowing.

Voice

I want a plain adult voice,
not any irony or not much
because that is just posturing,
mere chasing after effect.

What matters are those times
when you speak directly
to someone else or yourself,
clear-eyed and even-voiced.

That is the voice you will
learn to hear, there behind
all the other voices,

Unforced and open, speaking
clearly, articulating distinctly,
saying what is.

Marine Layer

Crows, cawing long and harsh and dark,
holding hard, they sway far and ride wide
in the wind-driven treetops back-lit black
against the dull white sky at day's end.

Sea wind sharp with redwood and bay,
pungent bright-bitter herbal green scents,
messages we know but cannot say,
and the old, cold salt smell of the sea.

Shade falls heavy on the hills' east height,
speeding cloud, the wind's rising rough hands,
the self-indexical gray and meaning light.

Wind increases, fog from the ocean dims
the deeps of the valleys, veils the hills.
The last sun in the west fails, night comes.

After Reading Quantum Theory

How after reading quantum theory,
even chairs and cups seem newly warm,
scented, dear as if our own flesh.
Stuff forms as subterranean upwellings,

Deep, blind structures emerging
shaped by rules of order binding
some basis yet below, where other
ever deeper rules grip and mesh.

So the starkly alien nature we only
half glimpse through the mathematics,
otherworldly ghost glint, taint of unreason,

Makes water, trees and rocks
our sisters, brothers, parents, family,
blood relation, one flesh.

Well-Articulated Before All Description

Dawn's growing light thickens shadow
into thing. Cold colors suffusing, diffuse
but brightening. Black line of fencerow,
curb and path and eave, homely shapes

Of garden tree and shed and house
in themselves mark no significance but
the world's entirely unhuman presence.
We may look, but what we see does not

Do fair by all this, things quite separate
from us. Were we to see truer, we would
acknowledge a plainer being than that

Which bears the burden of our intention
and our hearts, but calm, composed,
well-articulated before all description.

Nobska Beach

How true the shapes of the rocks,
New England gray granite emerging
massed in enormous, silent energy
up through the sand and the water.

How blue the sky, the sea, how sooth
the sun shining so warmly on our
hands and our backs as we come
newly wet from the water.

We here its creatures, immersed in
its own waters, dense salt-bitter
taste on our lips, considered touch

And lift of buoyant, enclosing liquid
as we swim sliding through it,
its comforts, its whispered words.

The Argument from Perfections

One of those metaphysically brilliant
new mornings with sun, and we do see.
Light exact, vision distinct, transcendent
one can think, as of some deep mystery

The precise, essential truth—but can't
say what, merely the morning, perfect.
Is that the perfection? Our world, our parent,
our ground? We its children, here, alert,

Pattern of its pattern, flesh of its flesh, we
at home here in this world, our own
very heaven? How could we not see,

Recognize it, life-force, almost will?
It loves us, we feel it, yet know then
too it's nothing personal—but still.

Mountain Home

Douglas fir forest spreading harsh and dark
across the mountain, bare winter branches
of ash and oak stark against the massing black.
Clouds flow down off the hills' higher reaches,

Lay bare the outthrust spines of the ridges,
slide off slow into the deeps of the valleys.
Here, cleared land and a line of old apple trees,
last remnants of house and fields and gardens.

The weak hill soil starves all, gardens and lives.
Poor, red hill soil, no nutrients only rocks,
all that labor giving a hard life, a poor return.

See here the ghosts of the man and the woman,
see here still the fading marks of their hands,
cutting and clearing and burning, all those trees.

Straightening Nails

"Poor people have poor ways" my grandfather
says as he sorts through his old lumber stacks
looking for a 2 by 4 a bit better than the one before.
Bad lumber is bad, "Won't last," he says, "just rots."

But he always looks, some old lumber is still sound.
Rough lumber was cheap then, but we were poor
so he searched and sorted, pulled nails and stacked.
Though not like kiln-dried clear, new from the planer.

Straightening nails, that was good. Hold it down
against the anvil bend-up, knock it straight
with three easy hammer taps, toss it in the can.

They're almost as good straightened as new-bought,
last as long, hold as well. They take more care
to drive but he could manage that. His hand was sure.

Picture of the Bride and Groom

The couple stands on a balcony with the greens
and sunlight of summer framing their good faces.
They are smiling out of the picture at us, happy
but a little frightened, husband and wife new-made.

We were there too, standing behind the camera,
also happy, smiling and clapping our good wishes,
supporters, friends, parents, family, the shared
strong emotions of love, and duty, and care.

We find these occasions, to pledge ourselves
to the bride and groom, their new life, and again
to each other, for we know it can only be so.

The construction of our lives is complicated past
understanding, a novel only a god could write,
but none did, it is ours, and we make it together.

Feeding the Quail

The day began in rain. The quail sheltered,
ventured out only later, becoming hungry
I suppose. The rain had then stopped,
the whole covey arrived and ate happily,

Sometimes standing up on tip-toe, flapping
their wings briskly, drying off, I think,
looking cheerful, sure. I am watching,
looking up from my philosophy book.

It will rain again soon, winter now tests
the time. Mild still, but the leaves color red
and fall, we need an extra blanket nights

And mornings it is dark late and evenings early.
The year turns, but feeling the good of the good
is anyway a person's clear duty.

Camellias in Spring

The camellias bloom again, profuse,
again spring comes. I hear small frogs
cheeking in the stream below the house,
see how intent the robins and crows,

Pressing and urgent needs of the new season.
The oaks are fresh with the greens of mosses,
visceral textures, a plushy prickle one can
magically perceive even at these distances.

It is only I, depressed or merely perverse,
who find gray and ash in the greening,
the frogs' busy sounds meaningless,

Harsh calls of robin and crow. Yet the fine reds,
the moist flesh of the blossoms speaking
and I hear, lucent pinks of opening flowers.

The Afternoon is Late, and the Light is Old

Wind is always about distance, and time's passing.
All day yesterday and all day today the wind
pushed and lifted and pressed the tree branches,
making them rustle and hum, but then shred, and clash.

And the line of the rooftree against the distant blue
of the far and grayed sky—the afternoon is late,
and the light is old, and sad, and cannot sustain life.
We see our deaths plainly before us in this light.

Wind is always about distance and time's passing,
so here near some end, we are thankful that it is
the day that ends, thank the earth's clock that says

The closing of the day has come, as it does,
bringing us calm for the night and, with the old
warm comfort of sleep, hope again in the morning.

The Falling Rain, the Slant of Light

Today I don't know what I'm doing,
I don't know what comes next.
I stand dazzled in the sun in the morning,
wet and blank in the rain falling soft

In the afternoon, and if there weren't
something in me that knows what to do,
I would stand stricken, emptied out
to a pure vacancy. But somebody is here who

Does know how to do things, and he
takes charge and finds the plan of the day.
I don't know him but I need him,

I think I would fail again and again to deduce
my tasks from falling rain, the light's slant play
as the sun moves across the earth's open face.

In One's Native Language

"Who's to know how to read sorrow rightly
or at all?" the poet asked, surely meaning
his own ignorance and all sorrows generally,
but his sorrow too, he must have meant.

As for me, since mostly I can't read it, since
mostly all I do is acquiesce unknowingly,
at home with my native words' meaning presence,
as a somewhat famous thinker said, darkly,

But about something else entirely. And you,
meaning to let the words mean what they do,
you to understand whatever you think you do,

And that's why the poet asked the question.
So now you, though it still won't construe,
but you'd already anyway decided to go on.

Antonello's St. Jerome

Antonello's St. Jerome is presented to us sleek
in court dress, palazzo classical and splendid.
We are shown the saint sitting at his desk
there in his studiolo, the artistically opened

Wall directing the sun to fall brilliant and slant
just on the book he is reading. We see him
as the painter sees him, a man for that light,
that civilized and civilizing book-filled room.

Not true to the saint, disdaining formal dress
went in dirt and animal skins, no care for civilizing.
Rather see him wild-haired shouting at the wilderness.

Rather see Antonello himself in the saint's library,
there among the books reading quietly, telling
us of scholarship, and thought, and a place to study.

The Vision of Reason

How a poem is more like
a syllogism than a novel,
someone said, and we know
what they meant.

Order, we seek it everywhere.
How it works is not clear,
pattern or likeness or rule or metaphor,
but we know it.

And order is very dear to us.
"Quod erat demonstrandum"
is just what a sonnet feels like or should.

Simple or not simple, all media, all methods,
even above narrative
it is the vision of reason we seek.

Right There All There

I'm padding along barefoot at night
on the way to turn down the heat,
feet familiar through dark rooms,
and I think that's all I'm doing.

But it's the embrace of all this, touch
of feet, planes of lighter darkness into
darker shadow, rectangles and cubes
of walls and rooms, felt densities

Of volumes of space in deeper shadow.
Then a sudden sharp, small enthusiasm,
some intense and compelling new thing,

The sense of the amazing possibility of it.
And for that moment, all at once, it is
right there, all there, clear and bright.

In This Open

It is or it isn't, or it was but it moved or it
changed or it ended. When you look again
it's something else, and we always look,
checking on what is as we step out our door.

I used to think there was no use in looking,
we without a clear and true way of seeing.
I was wrong, our poor means are enough
and we can begin from where we are.

For there might have been nothing, every
thing that might have been thus lacking is,
be not. No thing, no place, no space,

No where anywhere to show that loss.
But it is, it all is, and so we here,
standing in this open, do now see to see.

II

The Day Like a Struck Bell

Today there was a bell ringing all day
in the cold hard blue of the sky. Today
the sun was sharp but weak, and in the noon
warmed us but later the light was thin.

Today I did what was needed. Today
I feared, calculated, planned, struggled.
Today fear and strategy fought, and
fear won and calculation went awry.

Tomorrow will be harder, the effort greater.
I know. Nothing is allowed. Not allowed. Nothing.
Today the bell of the sun rang out.

Today I calculated, planned, feared, struggled.
Today the day rang like a struck bell,
the sound spreading through all things.

Even Only at the Office

Working days twist the soul oddly.
Money, status, place, we need to work,
attempt some success. Or, honorably,
because we want to do good work.

But the day moves and problems
press, and we struggle forward and press
back, and in the drama of our difficulties
the force of will we muster tempts us,

Makes us think we do important things,
makes us feel we are, even, somewhat heroic.
Conflict urges war's vocabularies

Even only at the office. But all untrue
and so is that feeling, cognitive trick,
and later we acknowledge we knew.

Tonight, and Again Tomorrow

It was late, tonight, before
the tension eased in my chest and
I could sit, quiet finally, give over
work and acknowledge day's end,

Able, although tomorrow would be
much the same as today,
to make a moderate peace
with the days before, the day

After. For it is wrong, I know,
to give tension of such an uncertain
basis houseroom, even though

Tomorrow it will all begin again
despite what I know,
or think, or where I go.

Failing to Find Your Public Face

To the just waking mind, dreams seem a crazed
commentary on daily life. After that kind of night,
you wake feeling obscurely shamed and lessened
because instead of adult purpose and clear thought,

The dream-self is all incompetence, disordered,
warped and only loosely strung together locally,
logical but weird, a calculus test with LSD mixed
in your morning fruit juice, a feel of perversity

In the mathematics, pornographic in a secret code.
Yet the day comes after the night, and the sleaze eases,
and you try to reassure yourself you only dreamed.

But on mornings like these, you just partly succeed,
so work threatens, ominous, and you leave home queasy
with a bad stomach and the vague urge to hide.

In That Felt Absence

I awaken taut at fierce, wordless sendings,
urgent silent voice. Walk the night-darkened
hall to the kitchen, start coffee, then stand,
looking out at the black. Regular doings

Helping to right the muddle of just waking.
Uncertain though clearing, my inner day
lightens and soon now I'll be able to say
"yes" to the new workday now approaching.

But once fully awake, I find I've lost both,
the night terror and that other thing,
unnamable, only faintly sensed, but truth.

So here, in this felt absence growing hard
and harder as I watch, see only the brightening
face of the new day becoming fully lighted.

On Being Anguished in Marin County

Of course it's not so bad, it's not
suffering like the great suffering
when all kill all and there is no safety
for the children and the houses burn.

I can read Z Herbert, C Milosc,
I know the difference, know
there is a greater world, terrible,
and I live in a green small corner.

No merit in that grand suffering,
smell of burning flesh and spirit,
honorable courage, no more.

But it's always there, the possibility.
We can't escape so we hide,
peering out through the leaves.

Political Poem

In order to understand how tolerance is a virtue,
consider sitting at table with a cousin, uncle,
even sister or brother, who professes some religion
or ideology negative, alien, utterly unbelievable to you

And the tenets of which, if implemented, would
coerce from you your self-regard and your rights
and force you to be a different person.
So if you and they cannot find how to disagree

And then move on to the weather, you will find
that in the end you can only move on to the
argument under arms. For tolerance is a virtue

That really only works well reciprocally,
and, seeing that, your sense of the orderability
of these things now weakens further.

What Happened Today

Snow fell steadily, firs in distant outline
dark ghosts behind the veiling white.
Winter birds, hungry, ate the food I offered.
Some dropped off their perches last night,

Food stores exhausted, falling dead
from hypothermia and starvation.
The birds now at my feeder made it through.
Eating rapidly, they prepare for tonight.

We sit in our warm house, looking out.
Sit quietly, in fear for our lives,
we are waiting for the vaccine.

Trump has been impeached a second time
but will not be convicted. Fauci says
all who want it vaccinated by July.

What We Do Hear and Don't

Some piercing sound, sliding past
the broken stubs of cypress branches,
through the marsh grasses, disturbing
the herons and the ducks, setting

The calm, bright fall day watching
out over the bay, setting the day at
edges and odds. And we, the people,
look at each other, fearful.

For though the day was bright, and
the coming light over the sea to our
eyes the edge of the light cone

To eternity, still we didn't see,
only the island across, and the piercing
sound, though meaningless, terrifying.

Reading the Medievals

"The real disillusionment," you said, "is knowing
enlightenment is real, the good life should be lived,
that duty and care are required of the rational being,
knowing that's all true and then feeling no different."

"You know the answer to that," I said,
"You told me last year when we read the Medievals.
If we were monks we'd be punished.
Acedia is a sin, acknowledging God but not caring."

It's not sloth, though we were being slothful,
talking and doubting and drinking beer.
It's knowing what the good is, and not caring.

But we were graduate students, not monks,
and we had to find for ourselves any presence.
"Have another beer," was all you said.

Here I Am Again

Here I am again
I say to myself,
wishing I knew
what I meant,

What it means,
the here, the now,
the this-ness looming
airy-massy.

What it means, I say,
but there's only
silence.

Order arises out of chaos,
leaves us here
conscious.

How After Darwin

If we now believe we know something
of what we are, thinking Darwin,
science, chemistry, brain cells,
neurophysiology,

Yet that does not tell the first, the founding
truth about us, how we do see,
each one for themselves,
lighted from inside,

How the world in that new light now showing
its additional dimension, and how
we, waking here

Alert but confused, though now newly knowing
this and each next moment
in this new life.

Kant and Freud

We all used to think that Freud told us
deep and important things about the self.
Though as you live with it, you find his
ghostly actors and intricate inner structures

Either absent ghosts or, for some sufferers,
haunting alien presences. But alien, other,
not-you, and having nothing to do
with your own fragile sense of self.

So Kant begins to seem "practical."
In dense, labored prose he assures you
of your self, determinate and distinct,

Secure, he says, in a transcendental unity.
But a formal unity merely, since on bad days
all that means is, the less unity the less self.

Aristotle and Newton

Aristotle tells us that each thing requires its sustaining cause,
the active principle which supports, realizes and continually
achieves, in each successive moment, each thing's existence.
All ordinary beings, we and all the world, are dependent,

Drawing our substance, lives and meaning from the prime source,
foundational mystery, being fully achieved and self-sustained.
We see ourselves caused and purposed by this first force,
see how we are imagined, defined, created, supported, enclosed.

Newton tells us that each thing continues in its motion unless
acted on by another thing, to change it. A barren landscape, unless
like Newton, faith in some unseen god somewhere outside the world.

Here no supporting, no succouring, no purposing, no reason.
After brooding about that, we see the last contingency, in us,
inescapable, created each time again when we ask "Why?"

The Wet Brown and Green

It all just goes on, memory is another world.
What does happen does,
reasons come after
and memory helps you find them.

Is that true? Or merely cynical?
The thing is, we can never
manage to understand
Why this? Why that?

Out of the earthen wet brown and green
past we came,
nothing, nothing was ever learned.

The images are too blurred,
you don't know, I don't know,
I say I don't.

Witness

The crows have been arriving this afternoon,
flying in, gathering.
Old friends and colleagues
talking sociably,

They caw and chuckle together
yet attentive to the day.
Maybe they expect a storm, or maybe
I just hadn't noticed before

And this is what they do every fall,
gathering on mild October afternoons,
alert yet tranquil,

Waiting to witness what comes,
winter, or (why do I think this?)
the end of the world.

Plague Poem with Climate Change

Hot, hot these summer days, strange and hot.
Things are changing. It's going to be worse
and then worse again, we all know that,
even if some deny it and the virus as well.

As if we feel Armageddon is what we deserve,
or else just what's inevitable. You love your
grandchildren but don't hold out much hope
for the world they'll come to live in.

We try to look for fixes, think who to blame,
but we don't get far. It feels inauthentic,
we're human and we're foolish and we know it.

It's the kind of thing we do to ourselves all the time.
Usually we get away with it, sort of, more or less,
but sometimes, as now, it goes really, really bad.

III

In Snow and Mountains

When you are strong, you think you can
look at dying alone, in cold and stone,
snow and mountain, think you can
look at it straight and see it done.

Lost there in snow and mountains,
feeling the cold and your body in the cold,
sun a hard bright white and you on skis
or snowshoes, warm, clothes sweated.

But the cold grips, and the body's center
though strong with its own combustion and warm
in the cold, is consuming its own matter.

So you imagine it, and then reach that part
where the body's richness is burnt up, all warm
has gone, and the cold begins to cut, and bite.

You Had Thought It Was a Unity

"You have to move on," you said,
knowing it was true.
You had thought it was a unity.
But who can follow that instruction? Can,

When it is time, turn your face away altogether
from what you had loved before,
can look to the left, to the right, pause,
then go in some quite new direction?

Go, and not look back?
And then do that again, and again,
and then again? Until that new direction

Is merely your death?
Only that? Really just
one thing and then another?

Turning Your Back

It's about sorrow and grief and endings,
places and people lost, projects unfinished,
things planted, shaped, cared about then gone,
the guilt and regret for what you did or didn't do.

You did your part, affirming and doing and making,
but none of it completes your life, prepares you for death,
eases, justifies, resolves, gives that calming sense
of well enough done you'd hoped for there at the end.

Soon all will be gone, for you cannot store up
good things achieved, beautiful things created and loved,
intent to hold against fate or death or the void.

None of it's additive, Arrow's Theorem's still true,
this calculus has no completing, countable or possible.
Turn your back and walk away.

How When a Very Bad Thing Happens

How a little before some
very bad thing happens
and you see it coming,
feel its terror growing

Stronger and stronger,
compression waves
squeezing you, crumpling
your heart, your gut.

And how when it arrives
you begin to live the
accumulating loss

Growing worse and worse
until it has all happened,
and then thereafter.

Bending Slowly Forward from the Waist

You flinch in an uneven motion, tilt
your head to one side with a kind of grimace, place
your hands against your abdomen, bow,
bending slowly forward and down.

You lean over your clasped hands.
The pain crawls and burns, in your heart, your gut,
a worm with teeth, chewing its way
through the soil of the body's substance, the soul's,

Good soil, being chewed and torn, leaking purple
or a cloudy blue-black.
Time passes and the pain recedes.

You slowly start thinking again,
sit, head bent, looking at your hands. Your face
feels stiff, and far away from you.

Pathology Report

Death speaks to me again today,
not joking now but in sober earnest.
My plan is obstruction and delay,
cancer the specific sign and implement.

Death. I address him respectfully,
"Death, Sir, what will you do with me?"
while doing all I can possibly
to push him altogether away from me.

I'll now have many conversations
with the keepers of death's practices,
verses, formulae, chemical benisons,

And I will learn from that syllabary's
truths the intricacies and inwardnesses,
the ways, attendants and ceremonies.

In Extremis

Your thoughts, circling, restive,
brush the edges of their container
as of rough pottery, abrasive,
but they are their own prisoner.

Your mind, flinching away tiredly,
loses focus on the point
but is drawn back repeatedly,
for you never really forget.

You don't believe in a finality
except at the extremis, reject
that looming mortality

So long as you have strength to resist.
Each day now goes and ends so.
Even when you sleep you know.

"But What If He Dies?"

"But what if he dies? What if he dies?"
my mind was screaming at me and I
cowered abused by the shouted fear.
I knew that voice. It was me.

As if one part of me heard and suffered
the other part's terror, yet I knew both,
I knew all, as if there were two, or even
three of us, dividing yet sharing the fear,

The one part of me screaming at the
others, the roar and shriek of the fear
shouted soundless, echoing, resonant,

The terror, crawling and growling.
"But what if he dies? What
if he dies?"

Aftermath

We look, and everywhere the edges and shapes
waver and blur. We ask to see things clearer,
in the open, but we cannot. Natural certainty, once
forcibly taken away, is not given back to us ever.

The past blurs across the lived present and felt future
of one's life's reach across time. Each day's meanings,
strung together roughly by hope, memory, nurture
and ordinary intention, are real enough in themselves,

But they each, they all, refer back to that signal event
and what remains is fracture and lesion, scab and scar,
the pain of the past written and bound and kept.

The long aftermath is not recovery, relief and rest,
but nagging unease, troubling dreams. Sometime later,
confused, we look at each other, suddenly bereft.

More Die of Heartbreak

More die of heartbreak, says the storyteller,
and we do. In our hurt, our fear, we see
the losses to come, knowing we will suffer
them. Wordless in our pain we grieve,

Saying again the old, worn words
of tears, and weeping, and crying out.
It is the seers, psalmists, the great past poets
moved blind to words who speak, shout

To be heard in the true voices, our own
voices, speaking. We call beseechingly
to the black sky, bow down in pain

And loss and grief. We wait, knowing our parts,
while the world crushes our bones slowly
and holds and then breaks our hearts.

Morning in Late Fall

Winter announces its coming modestly enough.
This year's leaves color and tatter, the apples
are done. The fall sasanquas are out now
and the japonicas show fully formed fat buds.

It was cold last night, we needed extra blankets.
I got up at seven to turn on the heat, but then
went back to bed while the house warmed.
It is now full day, morning passing, light clear.

And we think, behind the other thoughts,
how it is another winter that is coming, yes,
and will we survive, yes, but for how many more?

Though it isn't close enough for the question
to bite, just close enough to think to ask.
Noon comes, and the day continues clear.

Sensing and Sensed

Age buzzes and aches, phenomenal fact,
leaving only that faded eden, faintly remembered,
of a past perfect clearness of sense of a mind
washed clean and new-bright by sleep's night.

Nothing now washes me clean so purely
nor the mornings begin so easily,
opening into that state of grace and clarity
provided free of charge by the young body.

But I can still think, I can act, and, acting,
I do that and, if sufficiently distracted,
don't notice the exact thing gone missing,

Liquid happiness of perfectly clear sensing.
Yet this morning is itself limpid, liquid
happiness, is itself this perfectly clear being.

Again In the Rain

A northern city pressed down under clouds,
the neon black of streetlights on wet asphalt
and the substantive blackness of fir trees
in rain showing this particular embodiment.

One take on things, a certain set of meanings,
your personal, only past, the power of things
old and long-known compels. Though some places,
golden, then seemed to offer all those promises,

You're back here now, and not happily.
Not happily, you thought back then fifty
years ago either. But you can ever only

See a few things clearly, see them intact,
not many, the time is too short for many.
You can't learn a new life in a week's visit.

And We Walking Away

How we can, on some nights, go to bed to sleep
as if that were our sole duty and only thought,
hold our work and our lives still around us, sleep
the sleep of the quiet, the calmed, the dispossessed.

For on those nights, we have put by all our plans
and necessities, duties and futures, placed our selves
and souls in the hands of aging and death and fate
and the angels, as if they were there in nurse white.

We have set our souls afloat on the ocean of ending.
*But we need a better word than "senior citizen,"
or I do and you should!* I shout, old man ranting.

For it is a very demanding thing we do, the change,
the commitment, all those meanings to be reinterpreted,
dishes to be held balanced, and we walking away.

Hands' Desire

The part of me in my hands speaks to me,
urgent, saying plant, make, build.
My hands have strength to grip, though less,
even old hands still fit to the tool's handle.

The thing bright in imagination and desire
and the passion of the new beginning
held in potential in the hands, is a love
so old it is in the muscle-memory.

Yet my soul is tired now, as if sleeping
I lost forever the comfort of sleep.
A new morning refreshes me somewhat,

But it is the world reborn, not I.
Hands' desire doesn't end, though the soul
wavers, the loss lingers, and is not explained.

Sailing to Alexandria

We were born in randomness and chance,
evolutionary happenstance happening
to begin with one of our own, far sibling,
next mutation, though all, all innocents.

But the fates of those distant creatures
explains nothing, tells only the contingency
we already knew, no reason only vacancy,
emptiness, mere fact and nothing centers.

We are as if cast away onto the oceans,
perhaps-doomed travelers long on
a voyage from the west. Moral persons

Now, not innocents. Seeking Alexandria,
we desire then finally to begin to learn,
to study with Euclid, Plotinus, Hypatia.

Attending the Good

Nothing has changed but me.
I'm still old and I'll still die
but probably not today,
today I feel cheerful.

I woke into sunlight this morning,
though my nose still runs,
prostate still aches,
prosthetic hip still hurts.

None of that's changed,
days happen until they don't,
but if yesterday I saw

Only the bad and the dark,
today I will attend only
to the interesting and the good.

December 31st

It's the last day of the year, raining all day long.
I put on rain gear, go out back, walk around,
look at the bare fruit trees, the sodden garden soil.
I stop to consider the kale plants, small but vigorous.

The slugs don't like them, the winter only slows them,
when I eat them, I feel the virtue of really green greens.
Mount Tam stalls another cloud in from the ocean,
the rain grows harder. I sit on the porch, watch the rain,

The storm-pushed clouds, think about the new year.
It's already been celebrated in London, Paris,
by our troops in Baghdad. I'm old though, and I

Don't have to figure it all out, only a few things,
the pines pushed hard by the wind, fast-moving cloud,
black streaks of rain, the vacancy behind the rain.

Acknowledgments

Hands' Desire, Finishing Line (2020):

    Picture of the Bride and Groom

    Antonello's St. Jerome

    Reading the Medievals (earlier title: Accidia)

    Political Poem

    Kant and Freud

    Feeding the Quail

    The Afternoon is Late, and the Light is Old

    Right There, All There

    Tonight, and Again Tomorrow

    The Falling Rain, the Slant of Light

Michael Beebe earned a Ph.D. in Philosophy and then became a CPA to earn a living. He came to poetry later in life, when sometime in mid-life he found poetry was the only thing he could read, nothing else suitably serious, beautiful and truth-apt all together. Sometime then, also, he began to try to write poetry of his own. He now lives with his wife in retirement in the Portland, Oregon area. He reads philosophy and poetry and works at his writing. This is his eightieth year; he is now reading the poet Stanley Moss to learn how to be very old.

www.ingramcontent.com/pod-product-compliance
Lightning Source LLC
Chambersburg PA
CBHW020834110425
24863CB00003BA/236